# Contents

# People in the story

**Cristina Rinaldi**: works in the Museo Nacional de Bellas Artes in Buenos Aires, Argentina.

**Daniel Simeone**: gym manager at the Recoleta Health Club.

**Florencia**: receptionist at the Recoleta Health Club.

**Philippe Maudet**: director of a museum in Paris, France.

**Leonardo Martinez**: director of the Museo Nacional de Bellas Artes in Buenos Aires, Argentina.

**Roberto and Carlos Bocuzzi:** brothers and bank robbers.

**Cristina's parents**.

# Places in the story

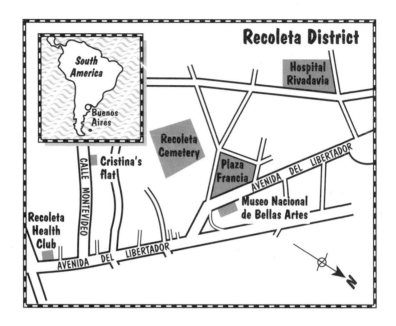

# Useful words

**Impressionism:** a style of art in France between 1865 and 1885. Some famous Impressionist painters are Monet, Pissarro, Renoir.

**Dulce de leche:** a sweet sauce made of milk and sugar.

**Tango:** an Argentine music and dance which started in Buenos Aires in the early 20th century.

**Churros:** bread-like cakes cooked in oil and covered in sugar.

Series editor: Philip Prowse

# *A Picture to Remember*

## Sarah Scott-Malden

CAMBRIDGE
UNIVERSITY PRESS

CAMBRIDGE UNIVERSITY PRESS

Cambridge, New York, Melbourne, Madrid, Cape Town, Singapore, São Paulo, Delhi, Dubai, Tokyo

Cambridge University Press
The Edinburgh Building, Cambridge CB2 8RU, UK

www.cambridge.org
Information on this title: www.cambridge.org/9780521664776

First published 1999
14th printing 2010

Printed in India by Replika Press Pvt. Ltd

*A catalogue record for this publication is available from the British Library*

ISBN 978-0-521-66477-6 Paperback
ISBN 978-0-521-79501-2 Book with Audio CD Pack

Illustration

# Chapter 1   *Cristina's motorbike*

At eleven o'clock one morning the director of the Museo Nacional de Bellas Artes in Buenos Aires, Leonardo Martinez, asked Cristina Rinaldi to come into his office.

'I want to talk to you about an important job I'd like you to do, Cristina. I think you'll be interested in it.'

'Of course. What is it?'

'A museum in Paris wants to send some Impressionist paintings to Buenos Aires. I spoke to the Paris museum director, Philippe Maudet, this morning and he's interested in using our museum to show the paintings. It's an important job. Would you like to do it?'

'Of course I would. Great! You know I'd love to see Impressionist paintings here in the museum,' answered Cristina.

'Good. I want you to begin work as soon as you can,' the director said. 'There is a lot you'll need to do.'

Cristina felt good all day. She loved Impressionist paintings. This new exhibition was wonderful. She couldn't wait to begin.

After work Cristina got onto her motorbike outside the museum. She was feeling good. She had an important new job, the sun was warm on her back and it was the start of spring weather in the city of Buenos Aires. Maybe tomorrow she could leave her jacket at home. This year September was warm, and people were already talking

about a hot summer. Cristina started her motorbike and
felt the warm air on her face as she rode along Avenida del
Libertador. She never wore a helmet because she liked the
feeling of the wind in her long hair. But her father didn't
know that. She remembered his words when he gave her
the new motorbike: 'always wear your helmet, Cristina –
every time you ride!' She hoped her father would never see
her without it.

Every day at this time Cristina rode down Avenida del Libertador to the gym at the Recoleta Health Club. Her day's work at the museum was finished and she was free. She usually forgot about her work as she rode down the Avenida. But today was a little different. She couldn't stop thinking about her new job.

Cristina began to slow down for the traffic lights. The traffic in the city centre was terrible. She didn't work far from the gym but the road had so many traffic lights. She stopped and looked into the car next to her. She saw two men in the car. She couldn't believe her eyes. One of the men had a gun. Then he looked out of the window at Cristina. She looked into his eyes, into his dark brown eyes and for a moment the man looked back. Then he turned his head and she saw a tattoo of a flower, a red poppy, on his neck.

Then she heard the sound of police cars. The man in the car lifted up his gun. Cristina felt afraid. She wanted to go quickly. She tried to start her bike but she couldn't. Everybody else was moving but she couldn't. Suddenly a taxi hit the back of her bike. She fell from the bike onto the front of the taxi and then down onto the road. Her head hit the road hard. She saw nothing, she felt nothing – she didn't even hear the sound of the ambulance which took her to hospital.

\*　　\*　　\*

Two hours later Cristina was lying in bed in hospital and her parents were waiting outside her room with a policeman.

'Where's her helmet?' asked Mr Rinaldi, Cristina's father. 'I know she had a helmet. She always wore a helmet.'

'She didn't come in here with a helmet,' the policeman told him.

'I can't believe it, she always wore her helmet,' Mr Rinaldi said.

'Maybe the helmet fell on the road, maybe the police left it there,' Mrs Rinaldi said quietly to her husband. 'It's OK. I'm sure she's going to be all right.'

They waited ten more minutes before the doctor came to see them.

'She's lucky,' the doctor said. 'She's going to be OK. You can see her now, but she doesn't remember anything about the accident.'

The doctor took them into the room where Cristina lay in bed. Cristina's mother and father began to cry.

'Are you sure she's OK?' they asked. 'Can't we take her home now?'

'No, it's better if she stays here for a few days,' said the doctor. Her mother stood by her bed.

'Come back and live with us, Cristina,' she said. 'It's not safe for you in the city. It's not only the traffic. We hear so many terrible things. Please, Cristina, your room is there for you. Come back and we'll look after you at home. You can change your job if it's too far to go.'

Cristina felt angry. She had her own flat in the city centre and her own life. She liked to look after herself. But her parents weren't happy about her staying in the flat on her own after the accident. Cristina couldn't believe her bad luck. She lay in bed listening to her parents.

Her father tried some other ideas. 'How about a flat with your brother, Cristina? He'd like it and he could look after you. Or maybe your mother could stay with you for some time. Just until you are better.'

But two days later she went back to her own flat alone.

She phoned the museum. 'I'm OK. I'll be back at work in a week,' she told the director. Her mother visited her every day and Cristina talked to her father every night on the phone. They agreed to let her keep her flat but there was something they disagreed with her about. They did not want her to keep the motorbike.

All of Cristina's family talked about Cristina's bad luck. 'It's the traffic in the city centre,' her aunt said when she phoned Cristina. 'It's the same at four in the afternoon and three in the morning.'

'Those taxi drivers go too fast and they don't look,' said her uncle who drove a bus through the city centre every day. The story of the accident was in the newspaper, a short story on the third page. Cristina's name and job were there but there was not a lot about the accident. Cristina's brother cut the story of her accident out of the newspaper and put it on the fridge in his flat. It wasn't every day that his sister was in the newspaper!

But Cristina herself was worried. She couldn't remember anything about the accident except the sun on her back when she was riding down Avenida del Libertador. But she wanted to remember. The police were still asking questions. The taxi driver said Cristina was sitting there on her motorbike in the centre of the road when the traffic lights were green.

The doctor said she was all right but Cristina felt strange – she got headaches – and she tried hard to remember what happened, to find answers, but she couldn't remember anything.

# Chapter 2  *A plan to kill*

In another area of the city, Roberto Bocuzzi and his brother, Carlos, were afraid. They were afraid that the woman on the motorbike who saw their faces would tell the police. Roberto and Carlos had $50,000 from a bank robbery and now they were rich. But they couldn't enjoy the money because the police were looking for them and this woman knew their faces. They didn't want her to tell the police. So they waited and made plans. They made plans to kill the woman on the motorbike.

*     *     *

A week after the accident Cristina went back to work. She felt better and she really wanted to go back to her new job as soon as possible. She only got a headache now at the end of the day when she was tired. Her mother stopped visiting her in the flat but she bought a lot of food. She put it in the fridge so that Cristina didn't have to go shopping for a few days. Cristina went back to her old life. She wanted to go back to the gym too but it was too early.

'Be careful for a week or two,' the doctor said. 'Don't do too much. Remember, you were lucky. You can't remember the accident, but it was a bad one. You lost your memory and you were lucky not to lose your life.'

For two weeks Cristina worked on the Impressionist exhibiton. She read a lot about the Paris museum and made plans for the director of the museum, Philippe Maudet, to visit Buenos Aires.

She took the bus to the museum in the morning now, or walked when she had time. She worked all day and then went home. She went to bed early and tried to rest a lot.

A few weeks after the accident Cristina went back to the Recoleta Health Club. She looked through the window into the office and smiled at the two people in there, Florencia and Daniel. Florencia was the receptionist and Daniel was the gym manager of the health club. Daniel was new there but he already looked at home in the gym. He spent most of his time in the office but he exercised a lot when the gym was closed to other people. He had blonde hair and blue eyes. Visitors to Argentina often talked about how many blonde, blue-eyed Argentines there were.

Cristina changed into her sports clothes and went into the gym. She only did a few exercises and then she went to have a shower. Daniel met her near the door.

'You're back,' he said. 'Were you on holiday?' Cristina didn't know what to say. She didn't think anybody knew she had been away.

'I had a motorbike accident,' she answered at last. 'I was in hospital for a short time.'

Daniel looked at her. 'Are you OK now?' he asked.

'I'm much better, but I only did a few exercises in the gym today. I still have to go slowly,' answered Cristina.

Daniel smiled and Cristina felt better. 'Be careful then,' he said and then he walked back to his office.

Cristina took a shower and thought about Daniel. She didn't know many people in the city centre – most of her friends lived near her parents' house – and she hoped Daniel would become a friend.

Cristina was tired that evening, but for the first time she

didn't have a headache. She could finally forget about the accident and start living again.

*    *    *

On the other side of the city, Roberto Bocuzzi also felt better. He and his brother, Carlos, bought all the newspapers from the day of the robbery and the motorbike accident and looked at them carefully. They read a lot of stories about the bank robbery and then, finally, they found a story about the motorbike accident. It said that the woman worked in the Museo Nacional de Bellas Artes . . . They now knew who the woman who saw them was.

Every morning for almost a week Roberto stood outside the museum and waited. But he didn't see her. Then, a week after the accident he saw a woman walking towards the museum. When she got nearer he saw that it was the woman he was waiting for. He remembered her long hair. He remembered her face. Roberto didn't want her to see him, but there were a lot of people in the street so it was not difficult to hide. She walked quickly past him and she didn't look at him. She walked through the door of the museum. Roberto looked at his watch. It was just before half past eight.

Roberto went to the bar behind the museum, the Café de Las Artes. He bought a cup of coffee and phoned his brother. Then he left the area quickly and took the bus home.

At three o'clock that afternoon Roberto left his flat again. At the bus stop near his home he waited for one of the colourful old city buses. The ride across the city centre was slow and uncomfortable but at four o'clock he was outside the museum. He saw Cristina leave the building at four thirty. He followed her along Avenida del Libertador. She walked so fast that he almost had to run. After about fifteen minutes Roberto watched Cristina walk in through some glass doors. Above the doors he saw the name "Recoleta Health Club" in red letters.

Roberto found a bar with tables outside. From his table he could see the door of the health club. He waited until he saw Cristina leave the gym and followed her home. He followed her for a few more days. He wanted to know if she did the same thing every day. He also wanted to visit the gym before he decided how to kill her.

# Chapter 3    *All the way from Paris*

Cristina's days were nearly always the same. She began work at the museum at eight thirty and left at four thirty. Then she went to the gym after work and stayed there for about an hour and a half. Then she went back home. She sometimes stopped at the supermarket on her way. Roberto and Carlos watched her for six days until their plan to kill her was ready.

Cristina, on the other hand, did not feel that her life was the same as before. The museum and her hours were the same but her work was very different. The new exhibition was keeping her very busy and she was very happy.

Cristina was sitting in her office when the phone rang.

'Hello, Museo Nacional de Bellas Artes, Cristina Rinaldi speaking.'

'Oh Cristina, hello.'

Cristina knew the French voice. 'Hello Philippe. How is everything?'

'Fine thank you. How are you?' asked Philippe.

'Great. When are you arriving?'

'On Wednesday. My plane arrives in Buenos Aires at nine fifteen in the morning. I'm travelling with Air France. The flight number is AF602. Will anyone be there to meet me?'

'Oh yes. I'll be there. I'll meet you and take you to your hotel. Then, when you're ready, you can come to the museum.'

'That's fine. Thank you, Cristina. I'm flying back to Paris on Monday so I'll have time to look around Buenos Aires a little – everyone tells me it's a beautiful city – so I'm going to be a tourist as well as a museum director!'

'Good idea. There's so much to see. I think you'll like it,' answered Cristina. She liked the sound of this man's voice. 'I'm looking forward to meeting you.'

'Me too. I'll see you at the airport on Wednesday.'

'Have a good flight.'

'Thank you. Good bye.'

Cristina put the phone down and looked at the picture of the Claude Monet painting she had on the wall in her office. When she was fifteen years old she went to France with her parents and fell in love with that painting with its field of red poppies. She went to see every Impressionist painting she could find in Paris. She spent hours in the museums and didn't want to leave Paris. Her parents understood then that she was serious about studying art at university. She kept the picture on the wall in her office because it made her feel good. She had the same picture on her bedroom wall. She often looked at it when she was thinking. But today she looked away from it quickly. There was something strange about the picture today. It didn't make her feel happy. It gave her a strange feeling inside. She didn't know why. Maybe it was because she was thinking so much about the new exhibition. An exhibition of thirty-seven paintings was a lot of work.

She had a lot to do before Philippe arrived on Wednesday. She took her notebook and left her office. She had to talk to somebody about the lights for the exhibition.

That afternoon she left the museum a little later than usual. Carlos Bocuzzi was still outside but he was getting tired of waiting. 'Maybe she went home early. Maybe she's ill. Maybe she's working late,' he thought to himself.

Just then Cristina came out of the museum and Carlos followed her. Cristina walked into Plaza Francia as usual but then stopped for a moment. She looked up at the white stone bodies of the monument in the centre of the Plaza. The French people who lived in Buenos Aires gave this monument to the city in 1910. This was the monument she could see from her office window in the museum across the street.

Now she was thinking about France and the French paintings that would soon be in the museum behind her. Carlos stood in the Plaza Francia. Most of the other people there were students from the university building behind the museum. They stood around in groups. They were waiting for friends and talking. In the park behind Carlos, the dog walkers of Buenos Aires were taking their dogs for their afternoon walk. Each girl or boy had seven or eight dogs that needed a walk morning and afternoon. It was often a job for young people who wanted to earn some money. They stopped at the flats in their area to get the dogs and then took them out to the city parks.

Carlos was watching Cristina and thinking. He was beginning to feel that he knew this girl and it was more difficult than before to think of killing her. But he knew that Roberto had a good plan.

'I mustn't be afraid,' Carlos thought to himself. 'Roberto is careful. He has thought of everything. Roberto has been to the gym three times, each time with different colour hair and different clothes. Now Roberto knew about day tickets to the gym and knew which machines and weights Cristina used. This evening Carlos didn't need to stay outside the gym and wait for Cristina. This evening Carlos could go home. It was the last time he had to follow Cristina – Roberto was going to kill her the next day. 'I must not be afraid. Only a few hours more,' he said to himself over and over again. Carlos was afraid but he felt sure that his brother would kill Cristina. Roberto was strong. 'That woman has to die,' Roberto told him every night.

# Chapter 4  *An accident in the gym*

The next evening, after work, Cristina was doing exercises in the gym. Twenty-eight, twenty-nine, thirty . . . her stomach began to hurt, but she did not stop. She was working hard. She wanted to feel as good as she did before the accident. She decided to stay longer that evening and do a few more exercises. She was finding it hard to stay in the flat in the evenings this week. She couldn't sit quietly and watch television or listen to music. In less than twenty-four hours she had to be at Ezeiza Airport and she had to be ready for every question Philippe Maudet could ask.

She looked around the gym. It was crowded and most of the machines were busy. There were more new health clubs in the city of Buenos Aires than new restaurants. Spring was especially busy as people were beginning to think of the summer and going to the beach.

Cristina went into the weights room. It wasn't crowded in there. You could always find a quiet place around five o'clock. Cristina chose her weight and lay on her back. She didn't look behind her but she knew that there was somebody else there. She closed her eyes and thought about her favourite painting, the one in her office. This usually helped her to lift the weight. She thought about that field of red flowers, but once again the picture in her head of the painting gave her a strange feeling. The red flowers made her feel afraid. She decided to think about home. That was better. After a few minutes she was ready to lift the heavy weight above her head.

Daniel, the gym manager, sat in his office looking out of the door towards the busy gym. He was thinking about Cristina. She was the kind of person he liked and he felt they could be friends. Daniel had a girlfriend in his home city of Rosario and he was finding life very quiet without her. He had a cousin in Buenos Aires and sometimes they went out for a pizza together and then went dancing on Friday or Saturday evenings. But Daniel wanted to find some friends of his own and start to build a life in the city centre. Cristina was the first person he wanted to make friends with. He wanted to ask her to go out for a pizza that weekend . . .

Suddenly, Daniel heard a shout. He got up quickly and ran out of his office. Somebody was hurt in the weights room. People were already there. Daniel looked down and saw the long black hair of the girl on the floor. It was Cristina.

'Are you OK?' Daniel asked. 'I'll call an ambulance.'

She wanted to get up. Her arm was hurt but she didn't want to stay on the floor. She got up slowly and moved away from the people.

'I'm OK,' she said to Daniel. 'I don't need anything. It's just my arm.'

Daniel took her slowly to his office and gave her a chair. 'Sit here and rest for a moment,' he said.

After a short time, Cristina looked a little better. 'I feel much better. I don't need an ambulance.'

'Are you sure?'

'I just want to go home,' Cristina said.

'OK, but could you tell me what happened?' Daniel said. 'It's important that I know.'

'I'm not really sure,' Cristina said quietly. 'I think the weight fell but I moved just in time. It hit my arm. Maybe it was too heavy for me.'

'Accidents do happen sometimes,' Daniel said. 'The important thing is that you're all right.' Daniel then went to look around the weights room. He looked at the heavy weight on the floor. 'Cristina must be strong,' he thought.

He went back to his office. He wasn't sure that Cristina was telling him everything about the accident. Her face was very white and she looked afraid.

'Are you sure the weight fell?' he asked.

'No, it didn't,' Cristina said quietly. 'Somebody pushed the weight. I saw it and moved just in time.'

'Could it be true that somebody wanted to hurt her?' Daniel thought. He wanted to find out who was in the gym that evening. Everybody who came to the gym showed their health club card to the receptionist and the number went into the computer. He could look at the computer and see who came in that day. He could also see how many day tickets were bought that morning. But he couldn't know who bought the day tickets. First, he needed to help Cristina home.

'Can I give you a ride home in my car?' he asked.

'No, thank you, I prefer to walk. The air will be good for me,' Cristina answered. Then she stood up. She didn't feel well. 'Maybe that ride is a good idea,' she said.

Before Daniel left the office, he spoke quickly to Florencia. He asked Florencia to try and remember anything she could about visitors to the gym that week. 'I'll be here early in the morning. Maybe you can tell me then what you remember,' he said to Florencia as he left the gym.

Cristina was a little afraid. She wasn't sure about going in Daniel's car. He looked kind and friendly but she didn't even know his full name. She was going to say that she wanted to walk, but then he said, 'Don't worry. I just want to be sure that you get home safely.'

Cristina got in. She wasn't afraid now. 'I think I've found my first friend in the city,' she thought as he drove her home.

# Chapter 5  *Looking good, feeling bad*

Cristina opened her eyes and looked at her watch. It was six thirty in the morning. She tried to move but she felt bad. She felt her arm. It was very difficult to move. She closed her eyes again. She couldn't believe it. It was a very important day for her but she couldn't get out of bed. It was now nearly seven o'clock and she still couldn't move her arm.

Any other day she could stay in bed, but not today. Philippe Maudet was arriving in Buenos Aires in less than three hours and she had to give a talk about the exhibition at the museum. She had to get up.

Her arm felt better after a shower but hurt when she brushed her hair. She went into the small kitchen in her flat and made a large cup of coffee. She didn't usually eat much breakfast but this morning she felt that she needed some. She found some bread in the cupboard and put some *dulce de leche* on it. The sweet taste was really good. She walked back into her bedroom. She was trying not to think about the accident but she couldn't stop. She looked at the clock and saw that it was time to get dressed. She didn't feel good but she wanted to look good. She tried on a short black skirt. It didn't feel comfortable. She usually wore that skirt to go out with her parents and it didn't feel right today. She tried on a brown suit and then a green jacket and skirt, but she wasn't happy with them either. At a quarter to eight she decided on a pair of black trousers and a white shirt.

She went back into her small kitchen. Her arm was hurting a lot again. She took some medicine and then she wrote down a number from the book near the phone. It was her doctor's phone number. 'Maybe I'll call later about my arm,' she said to herself. Then she left her flat and went to find a taxi.

*     *     *

On flight AF602 Philippe Maudet got up from his seat and walked down the plane towards the toilets. He didn't feel good. It was difficult to sleep on the long flight. He cleaned his teeth, shaved, and washed. That felt a little better. He went back to his seat and sat down to eat his breakfast. Only about two hours to go.

The man next to Philippe wanted to talk. Philippe smiled at him and answered questions about who he was and where he worked. The man was a Porteño: he was born in the city of Buenos Aires. He wanted to tell Philippe everything about Buenos Aires. They looked at a map of Buenos Aires while the man talked about his city and its buildings. He told Philippe about the different parts of the city that he must visit: La Boca with its colourful little street called Caminito, full of colour and life – the small metal houses there are blue, green, red and yellow and the painters work and show their paintings in the street.

He talked about San Telmo and its old buildings – in the restaurants and theatres of San Telmo you can see tango dancers and hear the real music of Buenos Aires. He talked about the Plaza de Mayo and the pink building, La Casa

Rosada, where the President of the country works. He talked about the shops and the nightlife. 'The city never sleeps: you can eat, drink and dance until the morning.'

They were arriving in Buenos Aires on 21 September, the first day of spring and Students' Day. On this day the students in Argentina begin their last part of the school year. Across the country the city centres are full of young people enjoying themselves. They walk around the parks and go to bars and restaurants.

Philippe was interested. He was looking forward to seeing Buenos Aires. People called it the "Paris of South America" and he was sure that he was going to like it.

\*     \*     \*

Roberto and Carlos Bocuzzi were still asleep at seven o'clock that morning. Roberto opened his eyes and remembered where he was. He remembered that Cristina Rinaldi was still alive. He closed his eyes again. He wanted to believe that he and Carlos were free, free to spend their money and live a good life without being afraid. He wanted to believe that Cristina was dead. But he remembered every moment of the evening before in the gym. He was using one of the weights in the weights room. Cristina was there in front of him, ready to lift a heavy weight. She was wearing grey shorts and a white T-shirt. She was slim and pretty. He could see her long dark hair around her head. Her eyes were closed. When she started to lift the weight, he moved nearer to her. When the weight was right above her head, he ran forward and pushed the weight down hard. She opened her eyes and looked at him. She saw the weight falling and moved just in time. The weight hit the floor. Then she shouted and people from the other room ran to her. Roberto left quickly and quietly. He remembered it all. He knew that she was still alive.

He got out of bed and walked into his brother's room. He wanted to talk. They needed a new plan.

# Chapter 6    *Meeting someone special*

Cristina got into a taxi at eight o'clock. It was only about thirty-five kilometres to the airport, but she knew there would be a lot of traffic. She sat in the back of the taxi and she thought about Philippe Maudet. What did he look like? She knew his voice well but she didn't know much else about him. In her bag she had a large piece of paper with "P. Maudet" written on it. She thought she would need it if the airport was very crowded.

She arrived at the airport early but she saw that the plane was also early. Philippe could be there at any moment. She found a good place to stand and she held the paper up in her hand. She watched and waited. After a few minutes, a man stopped in front of her and said, 'Cristina, thank you for coming. I'm very happy to meet you.'

The first thing she saw were two very dark brown eyes smiling at her. Cristina smiled at the young Frenchman standing in front of her. She shook the man's hand.

'How was your flight, Philippe? I'm sure you must be tired. We'll go to the hotel and you can rest before we go to the museum,' she said.

'No, no, that's not necessary,' replied Philippe. 'I'm fine and I want to see the museum. Let's go straight there. I'd just like a cup of coffee and then I'll be ready for work.'

There was a good coffee shop near the museum. They could get out of the taxi in Plaza Francia, thought Cristina, drink some coffee and then go into the museum.

Cristina liked Philippe. He seemed the kind of person she could enjoy spending time with. She had the feeling the day was going to be all right.

The taxi driver was waiting outside the airport building. The driver smiled at Cristina and put Philippe's small suitcase in the back of the taxi. Cristina and Philippe got in. The sun was just getting warm as the taxi turned into the Avenida del Libertador. Cristina could see Plaza Francia in front of them. She asked the taxi driver to stop. She then paid him while Philippe took his bag out of the taxi and found a table outside in the sun. He sat down and put on his sunglasses. He looked at all the young people around. He could see they were students and remembered that it was Students' Day.

Cristina turned around and looked at the good-looking man waiting for her at the table. She sat down and the waiter came to take their order. At a quarter past ten they were sitting with coffee and *churros*. They talked for some time about their lives and their work and their love of Impressionist paintings.

Cristina and Philippe spent the day in meetings with the museum director, Leonardo Martinez, and other people who worked at the museum. It didn't open to the public until half past twelve so they could have meetings and look around the museum easily.

Just before she had to give her talk Cristina ran to the toilets and took some medicine. Her arm was beginning to hurt badly, but she soon forgot about it as she talked about the exhibition.

She felt that Philippe was happy, but she couldn't talk to him very much at lunch. They walked to a restaurant,

Campos del Pilar, near the museum, with everybody from the meeting. They chose Argentine beef and watched while it cooked on the fire in the centre of the restaurant. Cristina was at the opposite end of the table to Philippe. She watched him talking and laughing with everybody. She could see that everybody liked him. She liked him too.

After the afternoon meeting, Philippe and Cristina were ready to leave the museum. Cristina was really very tired but she wanted to look after Philippe during his stay in Buenos Aires.

'How about dinner?' she asked.

Philippe smiled. 'I'm really sorry, but I'll have dinner in the hotel tonight, if it's OK. I'm so tired. I think I'll try and get some sleep. Can we go out tomorrow evening?'

'Of course,' Cristina said. 'I'll take you to the hotel now. We have a busy day tomorrow.'

'Thanks,' Philippe replied. 'Maybe after tomorrow's meeting, you can show me around your city a little. I'm looking forward to seeing it.'

Cristina took Philippe to his hotel in a taxi. 'See you tomorrow. I hope you sleep well,' she said. She watched him walk through the front doors of the Sheraton Hotel. She wanted to stay and talk to Philippe Maudet. She wanted to have dinner with him and find out more about him. She thought he was wonderful.

When Cristina got home she couldn't stop thinking about Philippe. She smiled to herself. She listened to her phone messages. There were two from Daniel. He wanted to know how she was feeling and he wanted to talk to her about the accident. 'Daniel is a nice man,' she thought. And she felt happy. She tried to forget about her arm but it was hurting badly again. She took some more medicine and sat on her bed. She looked up at the picture of red poppies in Monet's painting on the wall of her bedroom. The picture made her feel strange again. There was something wrong, but she didn't know what it was. She lay in bed for a long time before she fell asleep.

\*  \*  \*

There were two other people who couldn't sleep that night: Roberto and Carlos. They were talking. Roberto was angry with himself, but Carlos understood. 'I couldn't kill her myself,' he said. 'It's easy to talk about killing, it's a different thing to do it. We must make a new plan. A plan that's not so difficult. A plan where we don't have to go too near her ourselves.'

'But I almost did it,' Roberto said. He couldn't understand why he hadn't pushed the weight down harder. He had stopped for one second. In that second, Cristina had moved away from the falling weight.

# Chapter 7  *A bad night in town*

At seven o'clock the next morning the phone rang in Cristina's flat. It rang many times before Cristina answered. She took a long time to wake up.

'Hello. Who is it?' she asked at last.

'Cristina. It's me, Daniel. Are you OK? You didn't phone me back yesterday. Is everything all right?'

'Well, I'm fine, but I don't like this feeling that somebody is trying to hurt me.'

'That's why I'm phoning you. Do you want to go to the police with your story?'

'I don't think so. I know I saw the man in the gym who pushed the weight. But I don't think I could tell the police what he looks like. I don't know him.'

'OK,' Daniel said. 'But I'm worried about you, Cristina. Would you like to come to the club tonight and talk about it?'

'I'm sorry. I have to go out. But I can probably come to see you quickly after work,' Cristina said.

'OK. See you later, then,' Daniel answered.

'Thanks for thinking of me.' Cristina meant it. Daniel was very kind to her.

Cristina got ready and walked to the museum. She arrived a few minutes before eight thirty but it was not quiet. The museum was full of life. Cristina sat in her office for a moment. Three people looked in through the door at her.

'Hi, Cristina. Great talk yesterday.'

'Everything's going really well, Cristina.'

'Hi, Cris. Good luck today.'

There were smiling faces and kind words everywhere. She heard Philippe Maudet's voice outside her office and went out to meet him.

Cristina and Philippe spent another day in meetings. After lunch, Philippe showed the museum directors photographs of the paintings he wanted to bring to Buenos Aires. He had a photograph of the painting with the red poppies, the same painting that Cristina had in her office and her bedroom. Cristina took the photograph in her hand. Suddenly she felt cold and sick. She didn't know why. This was her favourite painting. It was strange that it was making her feel like this. She passed it quickly to the person on her left.

At half past five Philippe turned to Cristina and said, 'How about our walk around the city? Is it still OK?'

'Yes, of course. Do you need to go back to your hotel? I could meet you there if you want,' said Cristina.

'No, there's no need. Let's go now,' answered Philippe. He took his jacket and followed Cristina out of her office.

The two of them left the museum and walked down Avenida del Libertador. Cristina showed Philippe the Recoleta Cemetery. She told him the story of General San Martín who was the "Libertador", the man who made Argentina free.

'And there above the buildings and the trees you can see

the top of the English Tower,' Cristina said. 'It's the same as Big Ben in London. The British people who lived in Buenos Aires gave the tower to the city in 1910.' Philippe smiled. 'You'll want a tower like the Eiffel Tower from me before I leave,' Philippe said.

'No, I'll be happy with thirty-seven Impressionist paintings.' Cristina smiled and they walked on down the Avenida.

As they walked, Cristina decided to stop at the gym so that she could talk to Daniel quickly. Then they could get a taxi and drive around the centre a little. They could drive to Plaza de Mayo and see the famous buildings there, then come back to have a drink in a bar in the Plaza San Martin. After that they could walk on to the new area of Puerto Madero. She wanted to take Philippe to the restaurant where her father took her on the day she got the job at the museum. Then after dinner they could go to San Telmo and see a tango show at El Viejo Almacen. She couldn't let Philippe leave without hearing the real music of Argentina.

Soon they were outside the Recoleta Health Club.

'This is the gym I go to,' Cristina explained to Philippe. 'I had an accident in here two days ago and I need to talk to the manager for just a minute. Do you mind if we go in for a moment?' Cristina asked Philippe.

'That's fine. I'd be interested to see inside,' said Philippe.

They went in and walked past Florencia, the receptionist. She smiled at Cristina but stopped Philippe. 'Excuse me,' she said. 'I need to see your club card, if you don't mind.'

'He's a friend of mine,' said Cristina. 'We just wanted to talk to Daniel for a moment.'

'I'm sorry. That's OK,' said Florencia and she phoned Daniel's office to tell him he had visitors.

Cristina found Daniel and introduced him to Philippe. They talked for a moment about the gym and their jobs. Then Daniel turned to Cristina. 'I wanted to show you the names of people who came here in the last few days. The only problem is that we don't have the names of the people who bought day tickets.'

Cristina looked at the names but there was nobody she knew. 'I'm sure I don't know the man,' she said. 'I didn't see him clearly but I'm sure I don't know him.'

'OK,' said Daniel. 'Florencia isn't sure either, but I'll talk to some more people. Maybe somebody else saw this man.'

'Thanks, Daniel,' said Cristina. 'I'll see you soon.'

'Nice to meet you,' Philippe said to Daniel. Daniel shook his hand and smiled.

'And you,' he said. Daniel watched the two of them leave. He would like to be with someone tonight and thought about his girlfriend back in Rosario.

Cristina and Philippe walked out of the front door of the gym together. 'Let's get a taxi to the Plaza de Mayo from here,' said Cristina.

'OK, and on the way you must tell me more about this accident,' said Philippe. 'It sounds like a strange story.' They stopped at the side of the road to look for a taxi. There were always black and yellow taxis around but sometimes it was difficult for them to stop in the heavy traffic.

Suddenly an old Peugeot 504, which was parked on Avenida del Libertador, started and drove towards them. Cristina was looking for a taxi when she saw the Peugeot coming right at them. She shouted and pulled Philippe back from the road, but it was too late – the car hit Philippe and then drove away along the Avenida.

# Chapter 8  *Getting help*

An hour later Cristina was sitting on a chair in Philippe's hospital room. She was listening to the doctor, who was talking to Philippe. The doctor told Philippe that he was lucky. His leg was badly cut but not broken. The doctor's words gave Cristina a strange feeling. When she was in the hospital the doctor had used the same word: "lucky".

She stood up and looked out of the window. The street below looked the same as on any other day. 'Is it me?' she thought. 'Is it bad luck or is somebody really trying to hurt me?'

The doctor left and Cristina said, 'It wasn't a great evening in the city, I'm afraid. How are you feeling?'

There was no colour in Philippe's face. 'I'm OK,' he said quietly. He drank a little water from the glass by his bed. He looked at Cristina and tried to smile. 'I'm not sure why, but I don't think that was really an accident,' he said.

Cristina agreed. 'I've got a bad feeling too. We'll talk about it later. You must rest now. Is there anybody you want me to phone for you?'

'Don't worry. I'll phone the museum in Paris in the morning,' Philippe said.

Cristina wanted to kiss Philippe. His sad face looked so beautiful. She was falling in love and she knew it. But first she had to find out what was happening, why someone wanted to kill her and to stop them. She needed to speak to

Daniel. She walked quietly out of the room and went to look for the nearest phone box.

Cristina now felt that things were different. She could believe that she had had one accident in the gym but now this . . . ? She tried to think. Why would somebody want to kill her? She wasn't rich, she had no problems at work, she didn't know many people in the city centre. Why her?

She put some money into the phone and called the gym.

'Hi, Florencia. It's Cristina. Can I speak to Daniel please?'

'Of course,' Florencia said.

'Hi, Cristina. Daniel speaking.'

'Hello, Daniel. I'm sorry to phone you like this but I need your help. Did you see the accident outside the gym? My friend was hurt. Somebody tried to kill us, in a car. This time I'm sure. They drove straight at us. I'm at the hospital now. Philippe's hurt but nothing's broken.'

'Wait, wait. What happened?' Daniel asked. He sounded worried. 'I didn't see anything. I can't believe it. Are you sure somebody tried to kill you?'

'I know it's true this time. I'm sorry, Daniel. I need help. I'm really afraid now,' said Cristina.

'OK, Cristina. Just tell me where you are and I'll come and find you. Then we'll decide what to do next.'

Cristina gave him the name of the hospital and thanked him. Her hands felt cold and dry. She wanted to cry but she stopped herself. She went back to Philippe's room.

Daniel put down the phone but then he picked it up again. He phoned a friend of his cousin's who was a policeman. Daniel knew him quite well because he came to the gym twice a week. Daniel told the policeman the story about Cristina. He then told him that he was now going to get Cristina from the hospital and take her to the police station. The policeman thought for a moment and then asked him to change his plans. He told Daniel to take Cristina home. He believed that the man who wanted to kill her could try to follow her. Daniel agreed. He left his office and drove to the hospital.

In the hospital car park, Roberto and Carlos were sitting in a car talking. They knew that Cristina was in the hospital. They had followed the ambulance there and seen her get out with the man who hurt his leg.

'This time we'll get her,' Roberto said.

Carlos was getting more and more afraid. He wanted to leave the city and drive towards the north of Argentina. They had a cousin who lived in Tucuman, one thousand three hundred kilometres north of Buenos Aires. They could stay with him. But Roberto didn't want to leave until he knew Cristina was dead.

'The police will find her, Carlos, and she'll talk. Or maybe she has already talked to them and they are looking for us now. If we're in Buenos Aires, they'll find us. Too many people know us. Somebody will talk.'

Carlos knew his brother was right but he was afraid. 'So what do we do now, Roberto? How can we kill her?'

'We have to follow her and kill her – with a gun. We'll wait for her here. Then when she comes out, we'll follow her and we'll kill her. It doesn't have to look like an accident. We'll be quick. Nobody will see us. We'll just kill her.'

'I don't think I can do that,' said Carlos quietly.

'No, you drive the car, I'll do it. She has to leave this place at some time. We'll sit here until she does.'

\*     \*     \*

The brothers didn't see Daniel's car as he drove into the car park but they saw Cristina. She came out of the front door of the hospital and ran towards Daniel. The two of them went back inside the hospital.

'Come on, let's go and see Philippe and tell him where we'll be,' said Daniel.

'Where *will* we be?' asked Cristina.

'With the police.'

'You're a good friend, Daniel,' Cristina said as they walked to Philippe's room.

Daniel was like a family friend. Cristina couldn't believe it. In a very short time, two men had come into her life. One was now a very good friend and the other? She must wait and see.

Philippe looked a little better when they returned. He even smiled a little.

'Hi, Philippe,' Daniel said. 'I'm so sorry about the accident. I'm just going to take Cristina to talk to the police. I think she needs to tell them her story.'

Philippe agreed. 'I'll go back to the hotel as soon as I can. Don't come back here. It could be dangerous. I'll leave you a message when I'm back in my hotel room.'

'Be careful, Philippe. I'll come to the hotel when I hear from you,' Cristina said.

'I'll be OK. You be careful too. I'll need you to look after my paintings,' said Philippe.

# Chapter 9   *Remembering everything*

Cristina got into Daniel's car. 'We're going to the police, are we? Which police station?' she asked.

'We're going to your flat,' Daniel replied. 'The police will be there. They are hoping that the person who tried to kill you will follow us. They want to get him. We'll go down Avenida del Libertador.'

Daniel drove the car out of the hospital car park but he didn't see the blue Peugeot leave the car park behind them. Daniel turned into Avenida del Libertador. The blue Peugeot turned into the same road a few moments later and moved to the left hand side.

Cristina looked around her. She couldn't believe that less than a month before she was riding her motorbike down this Avenida every morning and every evening without a care in the world. Now she had no motorbike and lots of problems.

Daniel drove slowly through the heavy traffic. There were a lot of people around as usual. Many of them were on their way to have dinner in the restaurants of Recoleta. People in Buenos Aires never really have dinner before ten o'clock in the evening and the city centre was busy until at least three o'clock in the morning. All the traffic lights were red. It was always the same.

She looked at Daniel beside her. He looked tired and worried. He wanted to get Cristina to the police quickly.

He slowed down at some traffic lights as they were changing to red. Cristina turned her head and looked into the car next to them. She saw two men. The man who was driving the car was looking at the road in front of him. The man sitting next to him looked out of the window at Cristina. She looked into his eyes and she couldn't look away. She looked into the dark brown eyes of that man and for a moment he looked back. Then he turned his head and she saw the tattoo of the red poppy on his neck.

Suddenly Cristina remembered everything. She remembered the eyes of the man and the red flower on his neck, the poppy. She remembered the car and the sound of the police cars. She knew that these were the same men who had tried to kill her in the gym. The same men who had driven their car at Philippe. And then she remembered the gun. The same gun that the man was picking up now. The same man, the same gun. The same red flowers in the field of the painting she loved.

'Go, Daniel! Move! He's got a gun! He's going to kill us!' she shouted. Daniel drove through the red light and on down the Avenida. The other car followed. Daniel didn't have much time to think. He drove along the Avenida as fast as he could.

'What shall I do?' he asked Cristina.

'Turn into Calle Montevideo. We'll go past my flat. That's what the police wanted. I'm sure they'll be there,' answered Cristina.

The Peugeot was still following them. Daniel turned into Calle Montevideo. Cristina saw the two light and dark blue police cars parked across the road near her flat.

'Slow down, Daniel. Stop here. It's OK. We'll be OK.'

Daniel stopped the car suddenly and pushed Cristina down onto the floor of the car. The Peugeot behind was going so fast that Carlos couldn't stop it. He tried but the car turned right and left and right again. Then it hit one of the police cars and turned over. There was a lot of noise. People were shouting. Cristina wanted to look out but Daniel said, 'Stay there. It could still be dangerous.'

After another long minute it was quiet and two policemen came to open the door of Daniel's car.

'You can come out now. It's safe,' one of them said.

Then they heard the sound of an ambulance. It came into the street and stopped near the Peugeot. Cristina stood still. She didn't want to watch but she couldn't stop herself. The police pulled a body from the Peugeot. Cristina couldn't see if the man was alive or dead but she could see the blood. Men carried the body to the ambulance. When the door was closed, the ambulance drove off to the hospital. Cristina could see the other man, the man without the tattoo of a poppy, sitting in the police car.

*    *    *

Six months later Cristina was standing in the main room in the museum. It was the first night of the Impressionist exhibition. She was wearing a short black dress and her dark hair fell around her shoulders. Music was playing. Cristina looked around. Her parents were there, talking together and drinking champagne. Daniel was there with his girlfriend from Rosario.

After a few minutes the music stopped and everybody was quiet. They all stopped talking. Leonardo Martinez, the museum director, started to talk:

'Ladies and gentlemen. I am so pleased to welcome you

to this important Impressionist exhibition. We have never before had this number of Impressionist paintings in Buenos Aires . . .'

Cristina felt a hand on her arm. She knew that hand. It was Philippe. He had come back to Buenos Aires often while they were organising the exhibition and they had spent a lot of time together.

Philippe spoke quietly in Cristina's ear, 'It's really happening. Your parents and friends are here. The paintings are here. Monet's poppies are here. And we're here together to see them too.'

'I know. It's wonderful. I wish you and your paintings could stay here for ever.'

'No, I have to go home. But I want to ask you something. When I take my paintings home, will you come with me?'

Cristina smiled at him with love in her eyes and nodded her head.